S0-BSW-923

20 Instant
Math Learning Centers
Kids Will Love!

Reproducible Activities and Patterns That Help Young Learners
Practice Math Skills Independently

by Traci Ferguson Geiser, M.A.
and Krista Pettit

S C H O L A S T I C
PROFESSIONAL BOOKS

New York • Toronto • London • Auckland • Sydney
Mexico City • New Delhi • Hong Kong • Buenos Aires

Scholastic Inc. grants teachers permission to photocopy the reproducible templates from this book for classroom use.
No other part of this publication may be reproduced in whole or in part, or stored in a retrieval system, or transmitted in
any form or by any means, electronic, mechanical, photocopying, recording, or otherwise, without written permission of the
publisher. For information regarding permission, write to Scholastic Inc., 557 Broadway, New York, NY 10012.

Cover design by **Andrew Jenkins**
Interior design by **Holly Grundon**
Illustrations by **Rusty Fletcher** and **Maxie Chambliss**

ISBN 0-439-22729-1
Copyright © 2002 by Traci Ferguson Geiser and Krista Pettit
All rights reserved.
Printed in the U.S.A.

3 4 5 6 7 8 9 10   40   09 08 07 06 05 04 03

Contents

Introduction

Welcome to *20 Instant Math Learning Centers Kids Will Love!* This book is designed to help the busy teacher provide quality, hands-on, and developmentally appropriate math centers throughout the year.

Math centers offer kids opportunities to learn new concepts and practice important math skills—on their own! The centers reinforce essential math concepts such as number recognition, patterns, shapes, addition, subtraction, graphing, time, measurement, and beginning fraction concepts. Kids will make play-dough numbers and cookies, sort colorful bugs, measure objects around the classroom using an inch-worm ruler, graph animals, create a calendar, and so much more. They'll enjoy doing these super-fun, education-rich activities over and over again.

Creating an Instant Math Learning Center

Putting together an instant math center is easy! All you need is a pocket folder or manila envelope to store the materials you need for each center. This book provides you with almost everything else.

For each center, you'll find:

◆ **Materials list.** Most of the items in this list can easily be found in your classroom or home. For teachers working with limited resources, we've also included materials variations.

◆ **Student directions.** Written in easy-to-read language, the directions include simple, supporting illustrations to help kids work independently. Photocopy the

directions and tape them to the front of the center folder or envelope. (You may want to laminate the directions sheet before taping it to the folder or envelope.)

◆ **Procedure variations.** These suggestions help you adapt the center to meet the needs of each student. Find out how to make the center simpler for younger or struggling children, or more challenging for advanced students.

◆ **Reproducible templates and recording sheets.** Photocopy these ready-to-go templates onto white card-stock paper for durability. Cut and color the templates, then stick them inside the folder or envelope, along with any additional materials you may need.

Using the Centers

Before setting up a center, be sure to explain each activity clearly to children. We suggest presenting each center during a structured learning time, such as circle time. Show students how to use the center materials. If time permits, ask some students to demonstrate the center activity to assess their understanding of it.

Storing the Centers

You can use a banker's box or a plastic bin to store the centers. Use hanging folders with plastic tabs and labels to make it easy for kids to pull out the center they want.

We hope you and your students have a great time with these centers! Happy learning!

Count Your Cookies

Children use play dough to form numbers on paper plates. Then they make play-dough cookies and put the same amount of cookies on each plate as the number they formed.

Materials

- 10 paper plates
- Number Cutouts (pages 7–10)
- Play dough (Appendix A, page 109)
- A variety of cookie cutters*

* If cookie cutters are not available, have students roll the play dough into round cookies.

Getting Ready
Glue each number template to the center of a paper plate. Hint: Cover the numbers with clear contact paper to keep the play dough from sticking to them.

Make It Simpler!
Use numbers 1 to 5.

Challenge Them!
Use numbers greater than 10 (page 112) and smaller cookie cutters.

Count Your Cookies

To Do:

1. Choose one paper plate with a number.

2. Use play dough to form the number on the plate.

3. Make little play-dough cookies. You can roll the play dough into cookie shapes or use a cookie cutter. Put the correct number of cookies on the plate.

4. Do steps 1 to 3 again using the other paper plates.

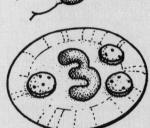

Number Cutouts

Number Cutouts

Number Cutouts

Number Cutouts

20 Instant Math Learning Centers Kids Will Love!

Laundry on the Line

Children hang numbered clothes on a clothesline in numerical order.

Materials

- Yarn or string tied between two chairs
- Clothespins
- Clothes Patterns* (pages 12–14)

* You can also use doll clothes or old socks (ask for donations or purchase some at a thrift store) instead of the paper clothes. Write or pin numbers on the doll clothes.

Getting Ready

Draw and place an arrow at the left end of the clothesline to show children where to start and in what direction to hang the clothes.

Make It Simpler!

Limit the number of clothes you use.

Challenge Them!

Cover the numbers on the clothes patterns before photocopying them. Then make several copies of the blank patterns and write higher numbers on them for more advanced students.

Laundry on the Line

To Do:

1. Look through the "laundry." Find the clothing with the number 1 on it.

2. Use a clothespin to hang the clothing on the clothesline.

3. Find the clothing with the next number. Hang it on the clothesline next to the first one. Keep going until all the numbered clothes are hanging in the right order.

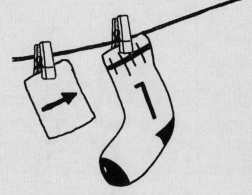

Clothes Patterns

Clothes Patterns

Clothes Patterns

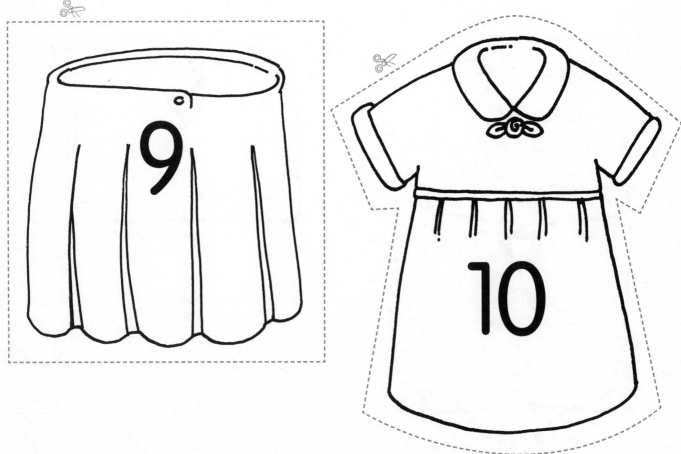

Create a Creature

Children draw a creature and its body parts based on the shape
on the Creature Feature Cards that they pick.

Materials

◆ Drawing paper*

◆ Crayons*

◆ Shape Cards (Appendix B, page 110)

◆ Creature Feature Cards (pages 16–17)

* You can also use white boards and dry-erase markers
  instead of paper and crayons.

Getting Ready

Sort the Creature Feature Cards according
to body parts (i.e., eyes, ears, nose, mouth,
legs, and arms).

Make It Simpler!

Cover the number on the Creature Feature
Cards before photocopying so children can
focus on the shape.

Challenge Them!

Invite children to create and use Creature
Feature and Shape Cards using more complicated shapes, such as a diamond, hexagon,
and so on.

Create a Creature

To Do:

1. Choose a Shape Card. Draw your Creature's body using the shape on the card. Make the body large enough so you can add body parts.

2. Pick a Creature Feature Card from one group. Look at the number, shape, and body part on the card. For example, if you picked a card with a 2, a circle, and an eye, draw 2 circular eyes on your Creature.

3. Choose another Creature Feature Card from a different group. Draw that body part on your Creature.

4. Do step 3 again until your Creature is complete.

Creature Feature Cards

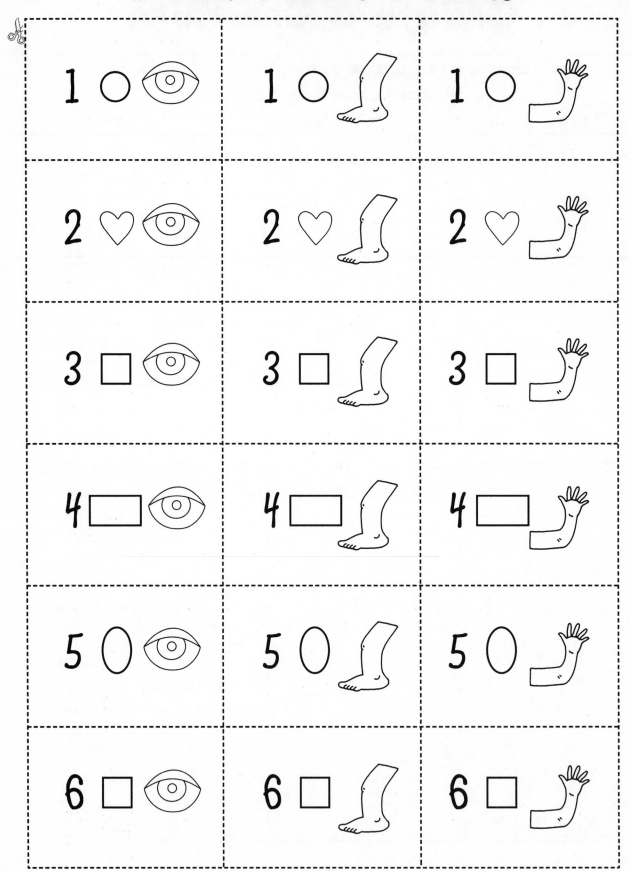

Creature Feature Cards

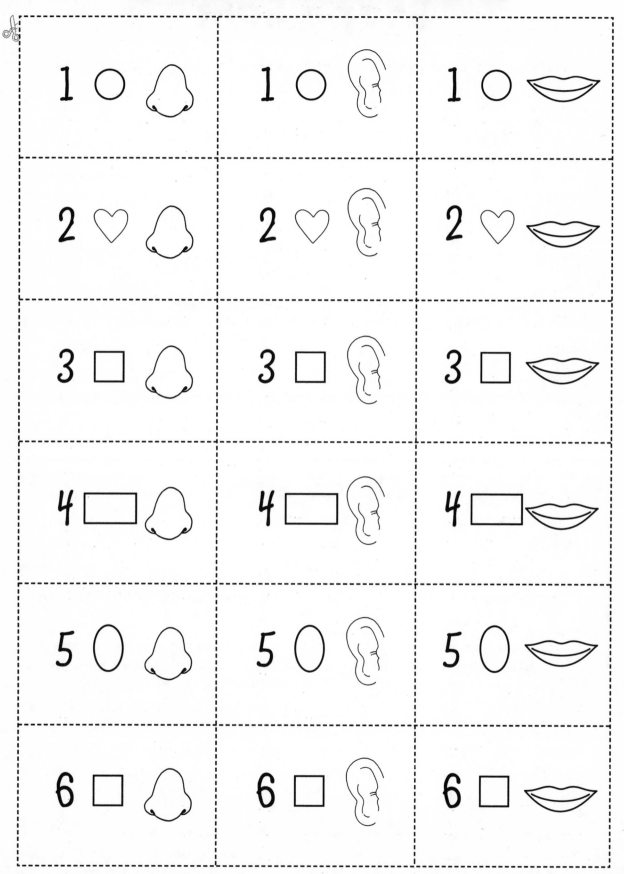

Shape Sort

Children sort Picture Cards into their corresponding Shape Sorting Mats.

Materials

- Shape Cards (Appendix B, page 110)
- Picture Cards (pages 19–20)
- 6 sheets 12- by 18-inch construction paper
- Magazines
- Scissors
- Tape

Getting Ready
To make Shape Sorting Mats, cut out the Shape Cards and tape each one to a large sheet of paper.

Make It Simpler!
Limit the number of Shape Sorting Mats and Picture Cards.

Challenge Them!
Invite children to draw new Picture Cards that can be sorted into each group.

Shape Sort

To Do:

1. Place the Shape Sorting Mats on the table.

2. Pick a Picture Card. What shape is the picture on the card? Place the card on the correct Shape Sorting Mat.

3. Keep sorting all the Picture Cards onto the correct Sorting Mats.

4. Look through the magazines. Find and cut out two pictures for each shape. Place the pictures on the correct Shape Sorting Mats.

pizza slice

Picture Cards

wheel	block	block
ball	sandwich	pizza slice
doughnut	rug	pyramid
orange	game board	cheese wedge
clock	book	mountain

Picture Cards

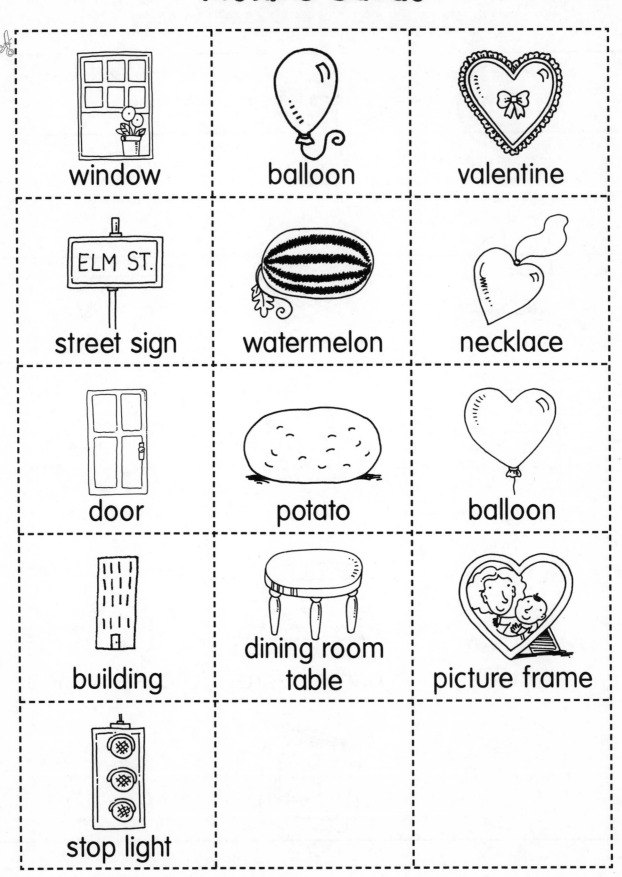

window

balloon

valentine

street sign

watermelon

necklace

door

potato

balloon

building

dining room table

picture frame

stop light

Land, Air, or Sea

Children sort transportation modes, animals, and objects according to where they belong—on land, in the air, or under the sea.

Materials

◆ Land, Air, and Sea Mats (pages 22–24)

◆ Transportation, Animal, and Object Cards (pages 25–27)

* If available, you may also want to provide toy cars and animals for the Mats.

Getting Ready
Color the Land, Sea, and Air Mats, as well as the Transportation, Animal, and Object Cards. Sort the cards according to their categories (i.e., transportation, animals, and objects).

Make It Simpler!
Give children only one category (e.g., animals) to sort.

Challenge Them!
Invite children to create their own environments, such as desert, forest, and so on, as well as appropriate Object Cards.

Land, Air, or Sea

To Do:

1. Place the Land, Air, and Sea Mats on the table.

2. Choose one group of cards, such as animals or transportation.

3. Look at each card. Where do you think it belongs—on land, in the air, or under the sea?

4. Place the card on the correct Mat.

5. When you're finished sorting your group of cards, pick another group.

6. Do steps 3 to 5 again.

Land Mat

Air Mat

Sea Mat

Transportation Cards

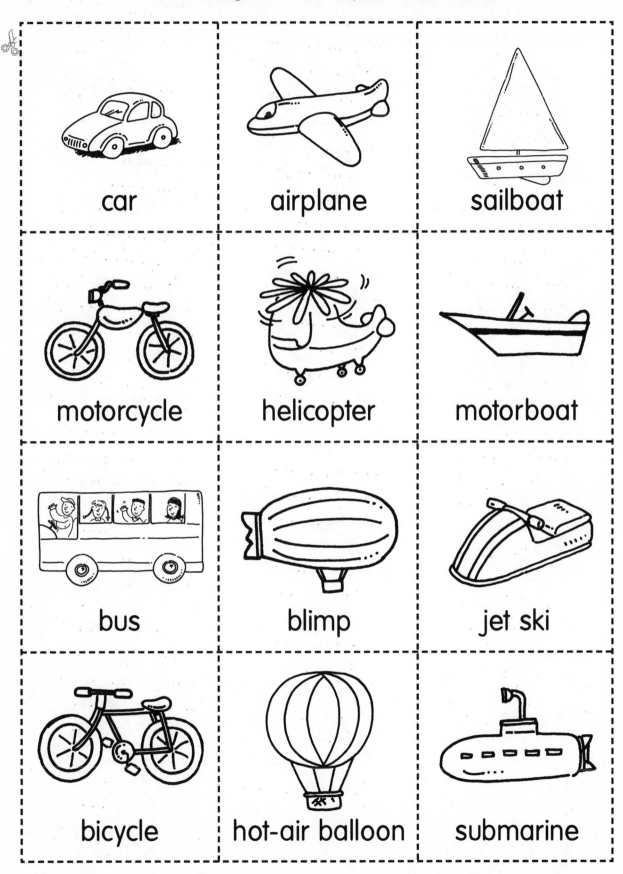

car

airplane

sailboat

motorcycle

helicopter

motorboat

bus

blimp

jet ski

bicycle

hot-air balloon

submarine

Animal Cards

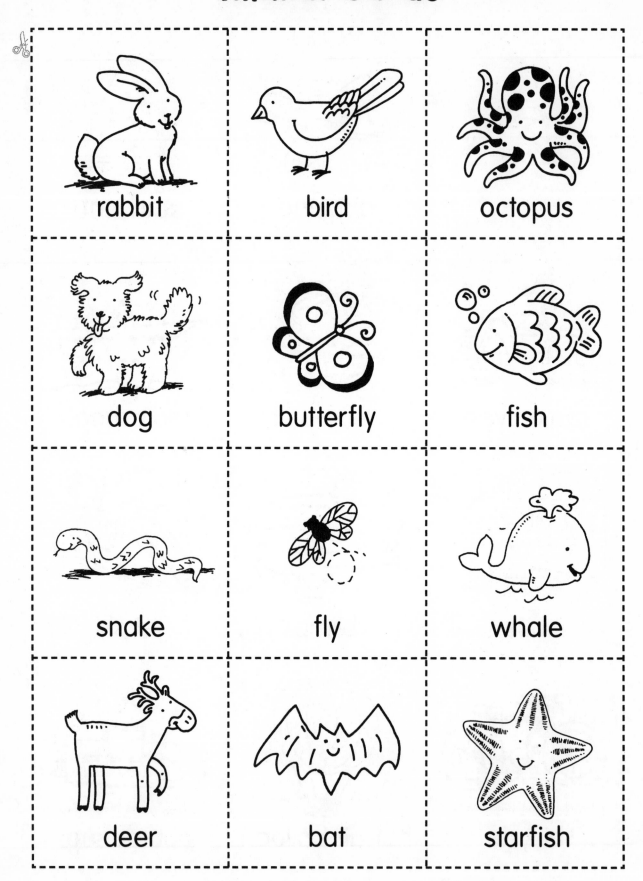

rabbit   bird   octopus

dog   butterfly   fish

snake   fly   whale

deer   bat   starfish

Object Cards

tree

clouds

seaweed

bush

sun

coral

flowers

kite

rocks

grass

rainbow

sunken ship

Bug-a-Boo

Children sort different bugs according to color, size, and presence of wings.

Materials

◆ Bug-a-Boo Cards (pages 29–30)

◆ Color Sorting Mat (page 31)

◆ Size Sorting Mat (page 32)

◆ Wings or No Wings Sorting Mat (page 33)

◆ Crayons or markers

Getting Ready
Color the Bug-a-Boo Cards and Color Sorting Mat as indicated.

Make It Simpler!
Limit the choices on the Sorting Mats. For example, cover the yellow and blue circles on the Color Sorting Mat so children sort only two colors. You'll also have to limit the bugs children use.

Challenge Them!
Have children create new Sorting Mats and organize the Bug-a-Boo Cards according to more than one characteristic, such as size AND shape, or wings/no wings AND color. Invite them to create new bugs to be sorted as well.

Bug-a-Boo

To Do:

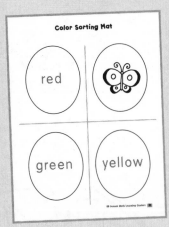

1. Place the Color Sorting Mat on the table.

2. Look at each Bug-a-Boo Card. What color is the bug? Where on the Color Sorting Mat does the card belong?

3. Sort the Bug-a-Boo Cards on the Color Sorting Mat.

4. After you have sorted all the cards, remove the cards and the mat.

5. Choose another mat. Sort the Bug-a-Boo Cards on the mat.

6. Do step 5 again with the third mat.

Bug-a-Boo Cards

Color these bugs blue.

Color these bugs red.

Bug-a-Boo Cards

Color these bugs green.

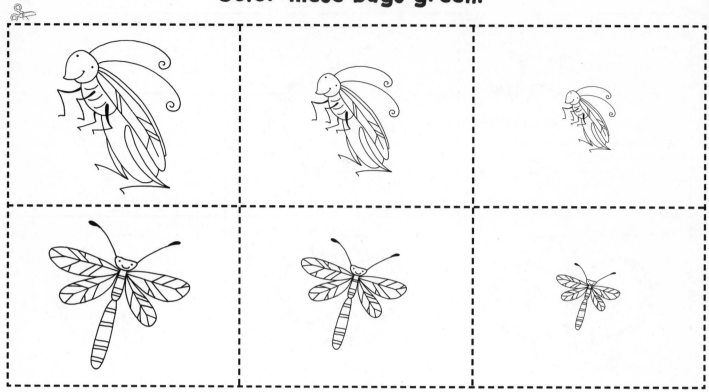

Color these bugs yellow.

Color Sorting Mat

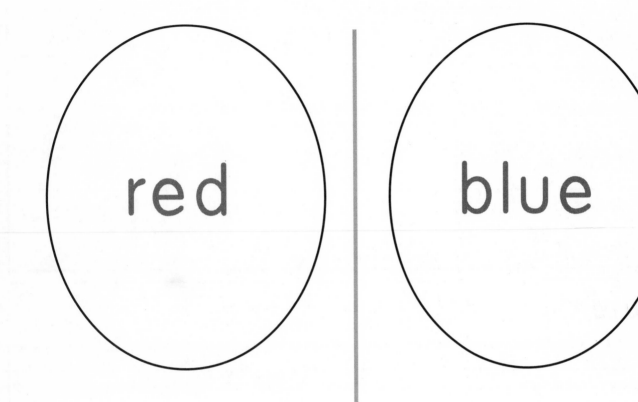

red

blue

green

yellow

Size Sorting Mat

Small

Medium

Large

Wings or No Wings Sorting Mat

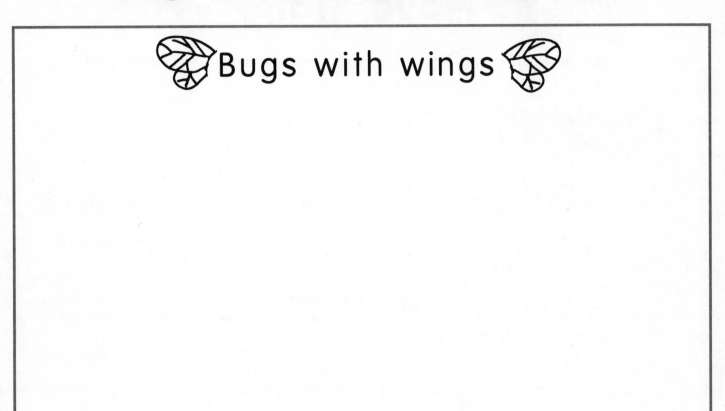

Bugs with wings

Bugs with no wings

Move Along

Children pick a Motion Pattern Card and follow the movements on the card.

Materials

◆ Motion Pattern Cards
(pages 35–36)

* If you prefer this to be a quiet activity, have children use a doll or paper doll to imitate each movement.

Getting Ready
Cut apart the Motion Pattern Cards.

Make It Simpler!
Before trying out the motions, invite children to verbally repeat the sequence several times. Then, have them say the activities while they are performing each movement.

Challenge Them!
Give children a blank sequence card and invite them to draw challenging motion patterns (e.g., AABCAABC or ABCDABCD) for friends to perform.

Move Along

To Do:

clap   clap   jump   clap   clap   jump

1. Choose a Motion Pattern Card.

2. Follow the movements shown on the card.

3. Do the movements again so you can feel the pattern.

4. Pick another Motion Pattern Card. Do steps 2 and 3 again.

Motion Pattern Cards

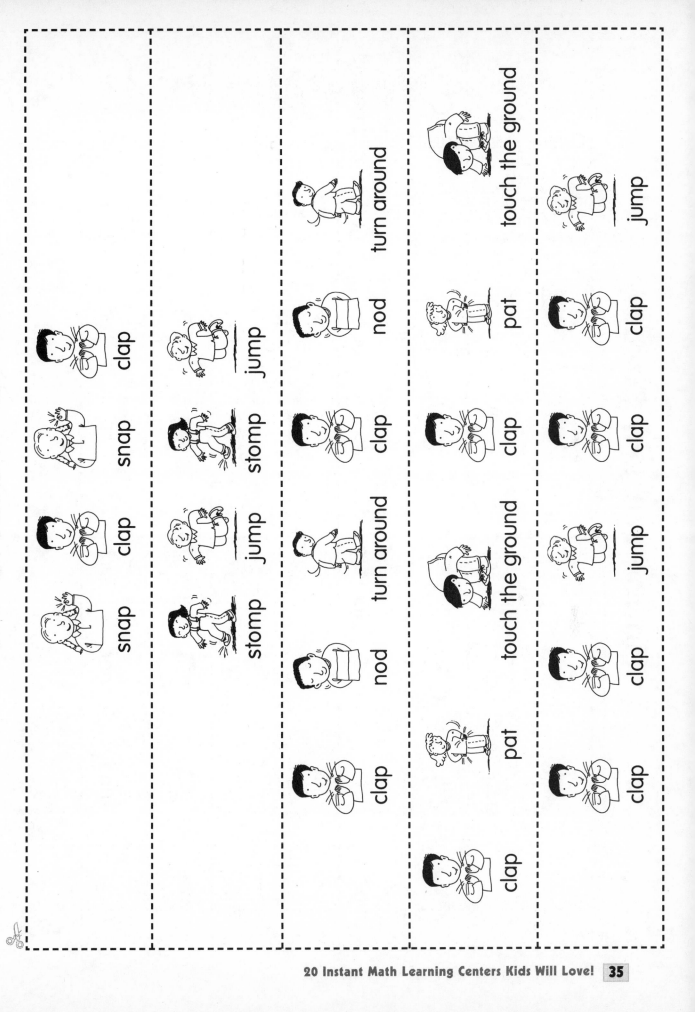

clap · snap · clap · snap

jump · stomp · jump · stomp

turn around · nod · clap · turn around · nod · clap

touch the ground · pat · clap · touch the ground · pat · clap

jump · clap · clap · jump · clap · clap

Motion Pattern Cards

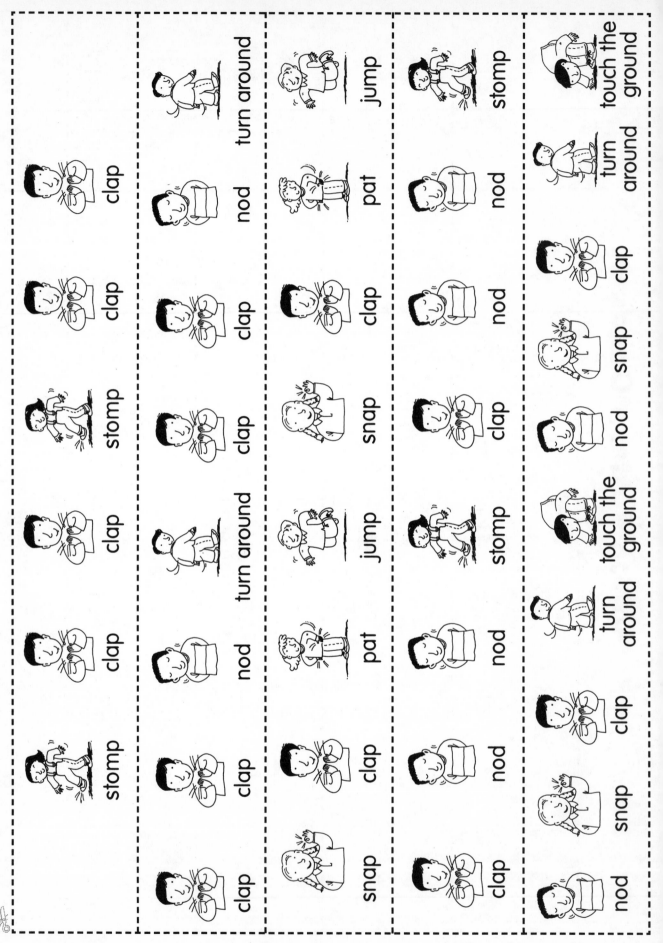

20 Instant Math Learning Centers Kids Will Love!

Pick a Pattern

Children follow simple shape patterns on Follow-the-Pattern Mats.

Materials

◆ Follow-the-Pattern Mats (pages 38–39)

◆ Shape Pattern Cards (page 40)

◆ Scissors

Getting Ready
Cut apart the Follow-the-Pattern Mats and the Shape Pattern Cards.

Make It Simpler!
Create your own simple patterns on pattern mats for children to copy.

Challenge Them!
Encourage children to create more complicated patterns using 5 or more cards.

Pick a Pattern

To Do:

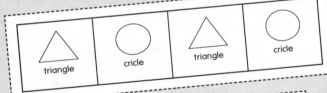

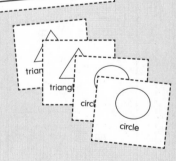

1. Place a Follow-the-Pattern Mat on the table.

2. Use the Shape Pattern Cards to match the shapes on the Follow-the-Pattern Mat. Repeat the pattern three times.

3. Remove the cards. Choose another Follow-the-Pattern Mat.

4. Do steps 2 and 3 again.

Follow-the-Pattern Mats

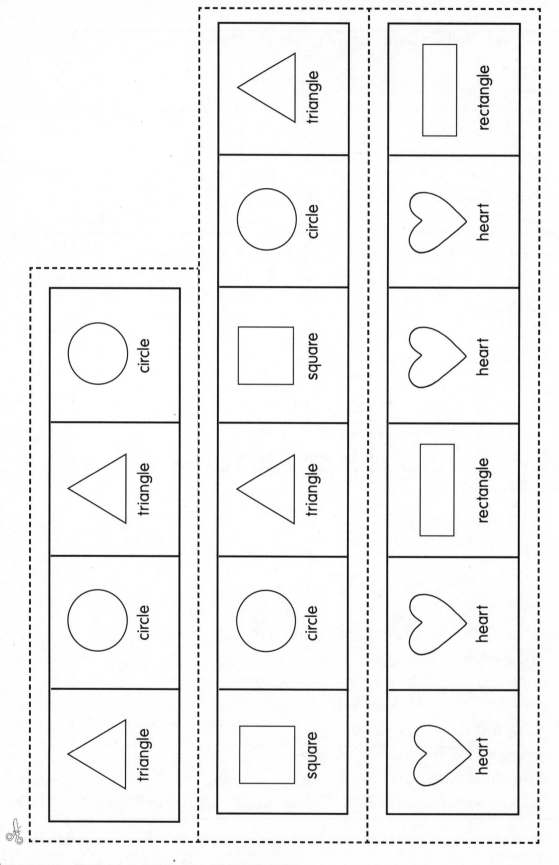

Follow-the-Pattern Mats

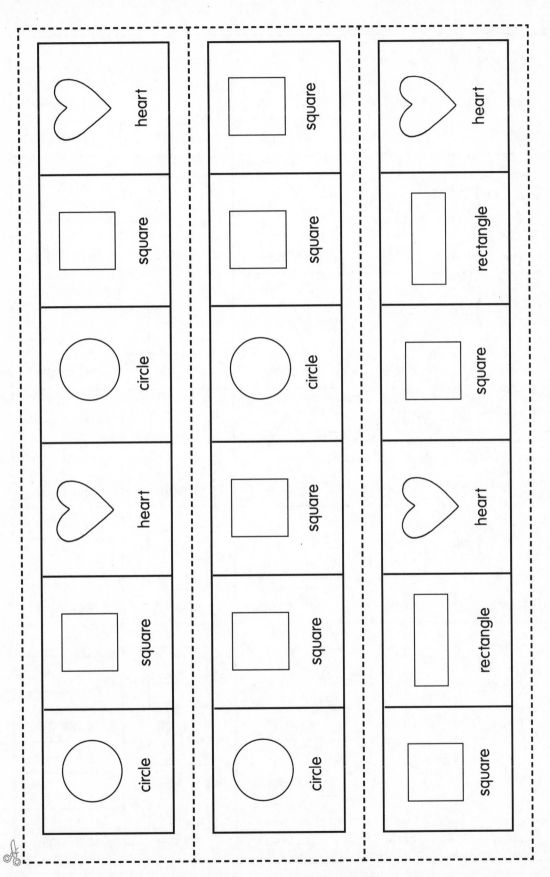

Shape Pattern Cards

heart	circle	triangle	square	rectangle
heart	circle	triangle	square	rectangle
heart	circle	triangle	square	rectangle
heart	circle	triangle	square	rectangle
heart	circle	triangle	square	rectangle
heart	circle	triangle	square	rectangle
heart	circle	triangle	square	rectangle

Measurement Madness

Children use various objects in the classroom to measure the Size-Up-the-Animal Cards.

Materials

- Size-Up-the-Animal Cards (page 42)
- My Measuring Sheet (page 43)
- Counting bears*
- Large paper clips*
- Chalkboard erasers*
- Crayons*

*If any of the measuring objects are not available, replace them with other objects in your classroom.

Getting Ready
Cut apart the Size-Up-the-Animal Cards.

Make It Simpler!
Use only larger objects to measure the Size-Up-the-Animal Cards. Omit the recording sheet.

Challenge Them!
Encourage children to use real rulers to measure the Size-Up-the-Animal Cards.

Measurement Madness

To Do:

1. Pick a Size-Up-the-Animal Card to measure.

2. Choose which object you want to use to measure the animal. For example, you can use the crayons to measure the fish.

3. Line up the objects next to each other to measure the animal.

4. Write your measurement on the My Measuring Sheet. Round up to the nearest whole number. For example, if the fish is 1½ crayons long, write 2 crayons next to the fish.

5. Pick another Animal Card. Do steps 2 to 4 again.

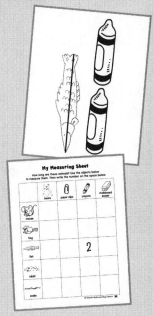

Size-Up-the-Animal Cards

My Measuring Sheet

How long are these animals? Use the objects below
to measure them. Then write the number on the space below.

	bears	paper clips	crayons	chalkboard erasers
mouse				
frog				
fish				
rabbit				
snake				

Inch Worms

Children measure different objects in the classroom using an Inch-Worm Ruler.

Materials

- Inch Worms (page 45)
- Inch-Worm Rulers (page 45)
- Scissors
- Glue sticks
- Objects to measure, such as board eraser, book, pencil, and so on*

* You can also cut out magazine pictures for children to measure.

Getting Ready
Cut apart the Inch Worms for children to use.

Make It Simpler!
Make the Inch-Worm Rulers ahead of time so children can concentrate on measuring.

Challenge Them!
Have students draw and record the objects they measured.

Inch Worms

To Do:

1. Glue an Inch Worm under each inch on the Inch-Worm Ruler.

2. Use the Inch-Worm Ruler to measure objects. Measure to the nearest inch.

1 inch	2 inches	3 inches	4 inches	5 inches	6 inches	7 inches	8 inches	9 inches	10 inches

1 inch	2 inches	3 inches	4 inches	5 inches	6 inches	7 inches	8 inches	9 inches	10 inches

1 inch	2 inches	3 inches	4 inches	5 inches	6 inches	7 inches	8 inches	9 inches	10 inches

Inch-Worm Rulers and Inch Worms

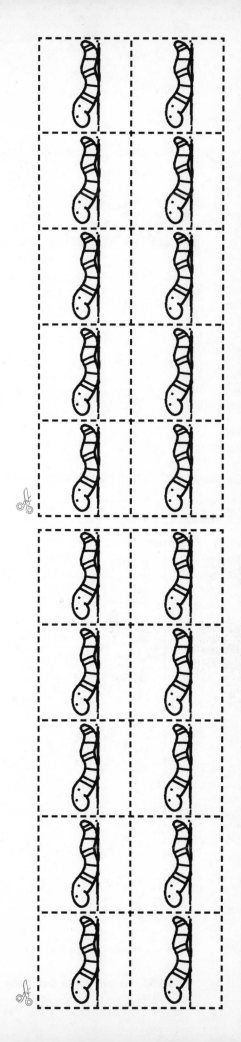

Graph This!

Children pick a Number Line and graph the numbers of beans on a Graphing Grid.

Materials

- Graphing Grid (page 47)
- Number Lines (pages 48–49)
- 100 beans*

* You can use markers, stickers, chips, small noodles, buttons, or stamps instead of beans.

Getting Ready
Cut apart the Number Lines.

Make It Simpler!
Create easier number lines using only the numbers 1 to 5 on blank patterns (page 49).

Challenge Them!
Create more difficult number lines on the blank patterns. Tape or glue two grids together for numbers greater than 12.

Graph This!

To Do:

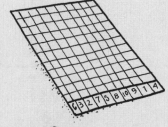

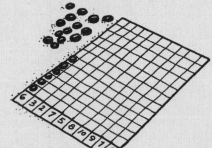

1. Choose a Number Line.

2. Place the Number Line below the Graphing Grid. Match the dot on the Number Line with the one on the grid.

3. Look at the number closest to the dot on the Number Line. How many beans should go on the graph above the number?

4. Place a bean on each square above the number. Count the beans until you reach the correct number.

5. Look at the next number. Do step 4 again.

6. Finish graphing all the numbers.

Graphing Grid

Number Lines

| 1 | 2 | 3 | 4 | 5 | 6 | 7 | 8 | 9 | 10 |

| 10 | 2 | 4 | 9 | 7 | 6 | 1 | 3 | 5 | 8 |

| 1 | 2 | 10 | 5 | 7 | 6 | 3 | 4 | 8 | 9 |

| 10 | 9 | 8 | 7 | 6 | 5 | 4 | 3 | 2 | 1 |

| 2 | 4 | 6 | 8 | 10 | 10 | 8 | 6 | 4 | 2 |

| 1 | 2 | 3 | 4 | 5 | 5 | 4 | 3 | 2 | 1 |

| 8 | 10 | 1 | 4 | 5 | 6 | 3 | 7 | 8 | 2 |

| 6 | 3 | 2 | 7 | 5 | 8 | 10 | 9 | 1 | 4 |

| 1 | 2 | 10 | 8 | 7 | 6 | 3 | 4 | 5 | 9 |

Number Lines

| 9 | 6 | 1 | 4 | 3 | 2 | 5 | 8 | 7 | 10 |

| 8 | 9 | 1 | 12 | 10 | 11 | 2 | 5 | 4 | 3 |

| 10 | 1 | 5 | 12 | 9 | 11 | 6 | 8 | 2 | 4 |

| 12 | 11 | 10 | 9 | 8 | 7 | 6 | 5 | 4 | 3 |

| 2 | 1 | 10 | 12 | 7 | 5 | 4 | 11 | 6 | 9 |

| 9 | 7 | 2 | 3 | 5 | 0 | 12 | 11 | 4 | 1 |

| 10 | 12 | 9 | 7 | 5 | 3 | 1 | 2 | 4 | 6 |

| 5 | 6 | 1 | 12 | 9 | 0 | 4 | 2 | 10 | 8 |

| | | | | | | | | | |

Graphing Fun

Children use Number Cards and Animal Cards to graph the correct number of animals on their Graphing Mats.

Materials

- Ocean, Farm, Forest, Zoo, and Pet Graphing Mats (pages 51, 53, 55, 57, 59)

- Ocean, Farm, Forest, Zoo, and Pet Animal Cards (pages 52, 54, 56, 58, 60)

- Number Cards 1 to 5 (Appendix C, page 111)

Getting Ready
Cut apart the Animal and Number Cards.

Make It Simpler!
Limit the Number and Animal Cards so children graph only 2 or 3 items.

Challenge Them!
Encourage children to ask each other (verbally or in writing) questions about their graphs.

Graphing Fun

To Do:

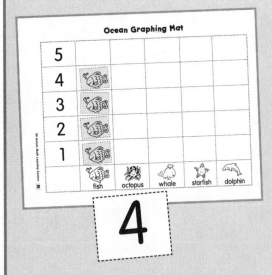

1. Choose a Graphing Mat and its matching set of Animal Cards.

2. Pick a Number Card for the first animal shown on the Graphing Mat.

3. Place that number of Animal Cards on the Graphing Mat above the animal's picture.

4. Do steps 2 and 3 again with the next animal on the Graphing Mat. Keep going until all the animals have been graphed.

5. Remove the cards. Do steps 1 to 4 again using a different Graphing Mat and its Animal Cards.

Ocean Graphing Mat

	fish	octopus	whale	starfish	dolphin
5					
4					
3					
2					
1					

Ocean Animal Cards

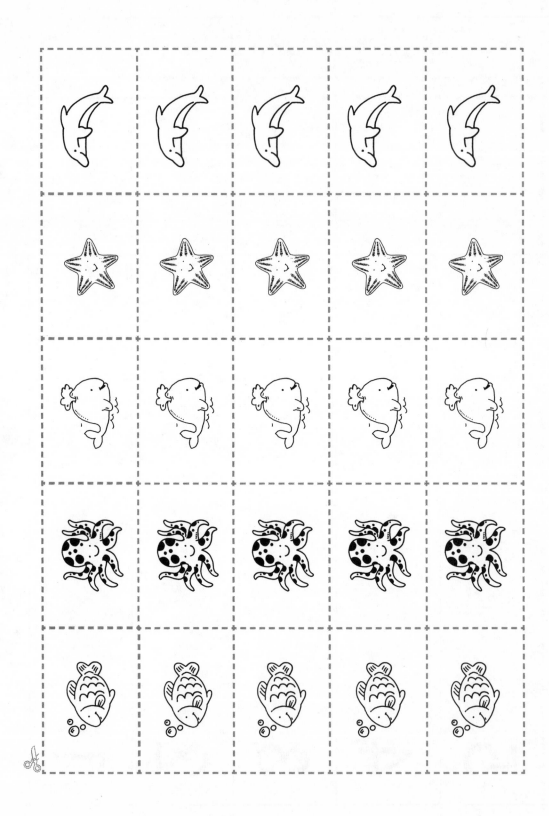

Farm Graphing Mat

5					
4					
3					
2					
1					
	cow	horse	pig	duck	sheep

Farm Animal Cards

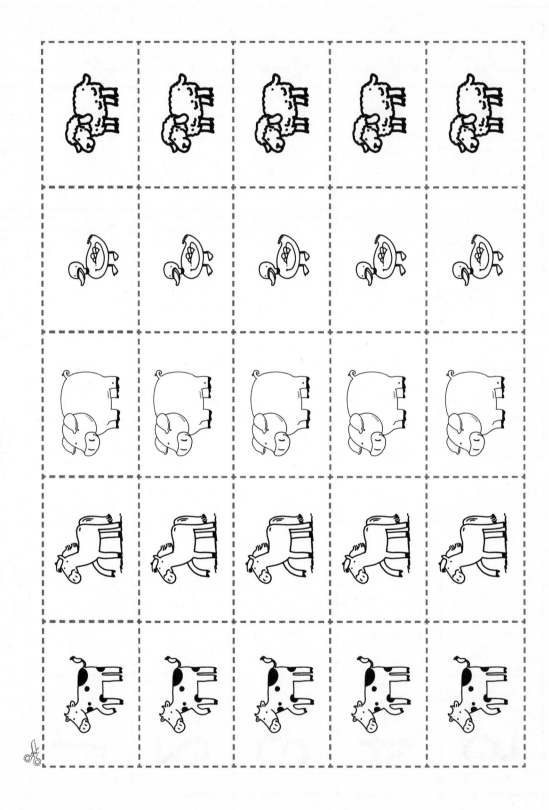

Forest Graphing Mat

5					
4					
3					
2					
1					
	bear	cougar	squirrel	raccoon	rabbit

Forest Animal Cards

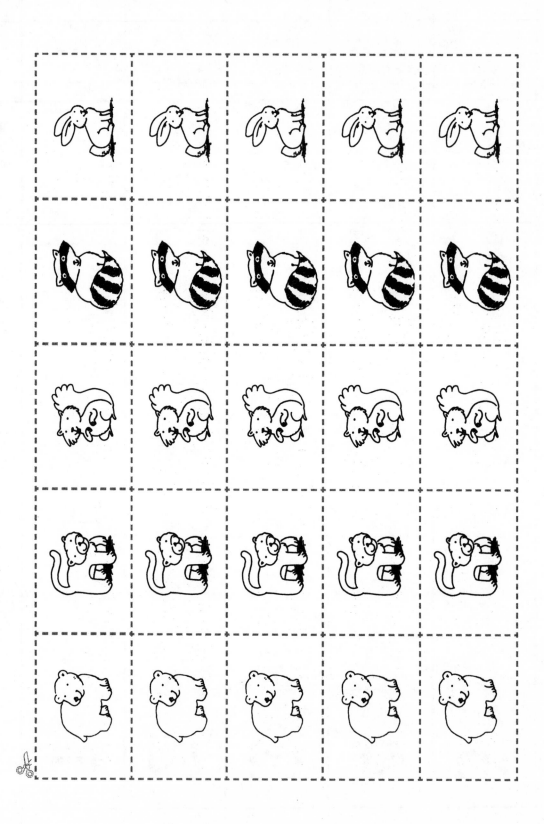

Zoo Graphing Mat

	elephant	lion	zebra	giraffe	tiger
5					
4					
3					
2					
1					

Zoo Animal Cards

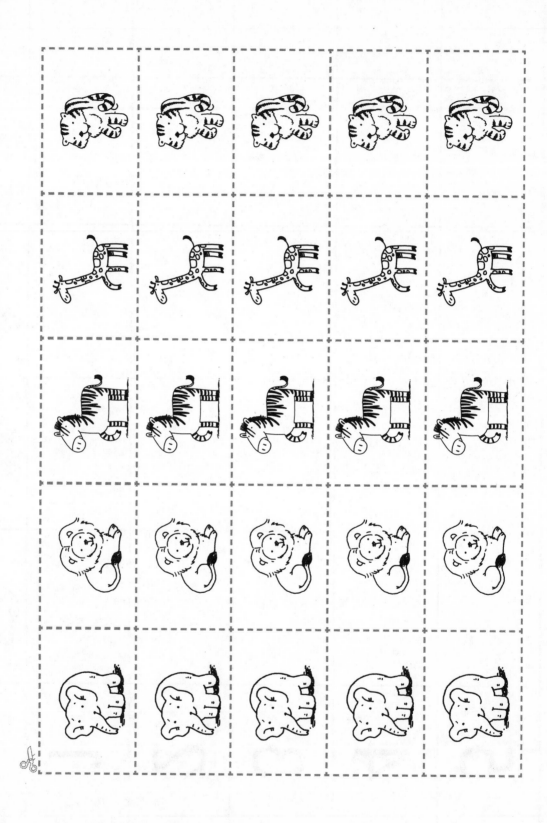

20 Instant Math Learning Centers Kids Will Love!

Pet Graphing Mat

5					
4					
3					
2					
1					
	dog	cat	gerbil	snake	bird

Pet Animal Cards

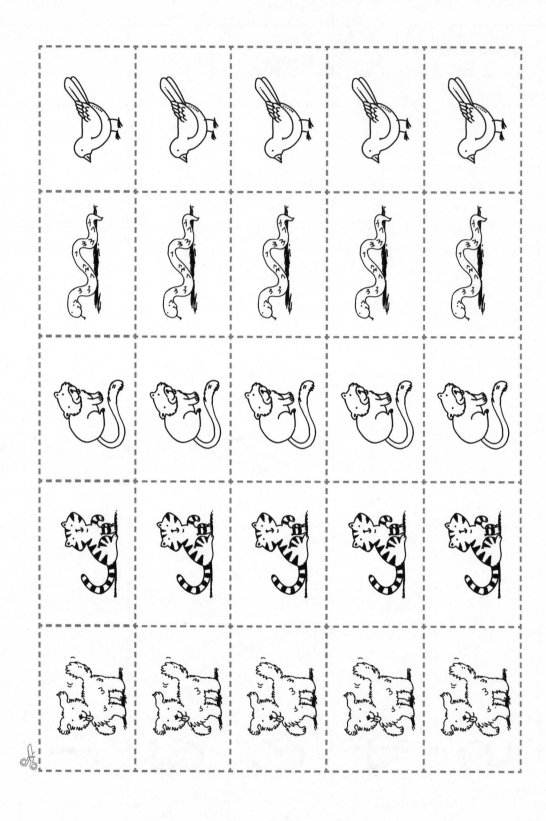

20 Instant Math Learning Centers Kids Will Love!

Lunch Orders to Go

Children read a Lunch Order Card and fill a plastic bag with Food Items based on the order. Then, they add up the Food Items in the bag.

Materials

- Plastic sandwich bags
- 10 copies of Food Items (page 62)
- Lunch Order Cards (pages 63–64)
- Pencils or dry-erase markers

Getting Ready
Laminate the Lunch Order Cards and have students use dry-erase markers so the cards can be reused.

Make It Simpler!
Limit the items on the Lunch Order Card by covering some items. You can also write simpler orders on blank Order Cards (page 64).

Challenge Them!
Invite students to make and fill their own Lunch Order Forms.

Lunch Orders to Go

To Do:

1. Take a plastic sandwich bag. Choose a Lunch Order Card.

2. Look at the first food on the card. How many were ordered?

3. Place the correct number of the Food Item in the bag. Put a check next to the food on the card.

4. Look at the next item on the card. Do step 3 again.

5. Keep adding Food Items in the bag until the order is complete.

6. Count the number of Food Items in the bag. Write the number next to "Total."

7. Empty the bag and choose a different Lunch Order Card. Do steps 2 to 6 again.

Food Items

Lunch Order Cards

✓		Lunch Order #1
	1	(sandwich)
	1	(banana)
	1	(milk)
	1	(orange)
	1	(chips)
	0	(apple)
		Total

✓		Lunch Order #2
	2	(orange)
	1	(sandwich)
	0	(chips)
	1	(milk)
	1	(apple)
	0	(banana)
		Total

✓		Lunch Order #3
	2	(banana)
	0	(orange)
	0	(apple)
	2	(chips)
	0	(milk)
	2	(sandwich)
		Total

✓		Lunch Order #4
	2	(milk)
	3	(sandwich)
	1	(banana)
	1	(apple)
	1	(chips)
	3	(orange)
		Total

Lunch Order Cards

✓		Lunch Order #5
	1	🍌
	4	🥪
	2	CHIPS
	3	🍊
	4	MILK
	0	🍎
		Total

✓		Lunch Order #6
	3	🍊
	4	MILK
	2	🍎
	4	🍌
	3	CHIPS
	5	🥪
		Total

✓		Lunch Order #7
	5	🍊
	3	🥪
	2	CHIPS
	4	🍌
	3	🍎
	2	MILK
		Total

✓		Lunch Order #8
		Total

Spotting the Animals

Children roll a die two times to find out how many spots (buttons) to put on an Animal Addition Card. Then, they add up the spots on the animal.

Materials

- Animal Addition Cards (pages 66–69)
- A die
- 2 different colors of buttons*

- 2 copies of Number Cards 1 to 12 (Appendix C, pages 111–112)

*If buttons are not available, use two different colors of torn paper, plastic chips, coins, beans, etc.

Make It Simpler!

Cover the letters on the Animal Addition Cards before photocopying them. Write numbers in the addition boxes. Have children put the correct number of spots on the animal and find the sum without rolling the die.

Challenge Them!

Have children roll two dice at the same time for the numbers they need to add. Use the Number Cards 2 to 20.

Spotting the Animals

To Do:

1. Choose an Animal Addition Card.

2. Roll the die. Find the Number Card that matches the number on the die. Place it in box A of the Animal Addition Card.

3. Put the correct number of buttons on the animal. Use only one color of buttons.

4. Do step 2 again. This time, put the Number Card in box B.

5. Put the correct number of buttons on the animal. Use the other color.

6. Count all the buttons. Place the matching Number Card in box C.

7. Remove the buttons. Do steps 2 to 6 again with another Animal Addition Card.

Animal Addition Card

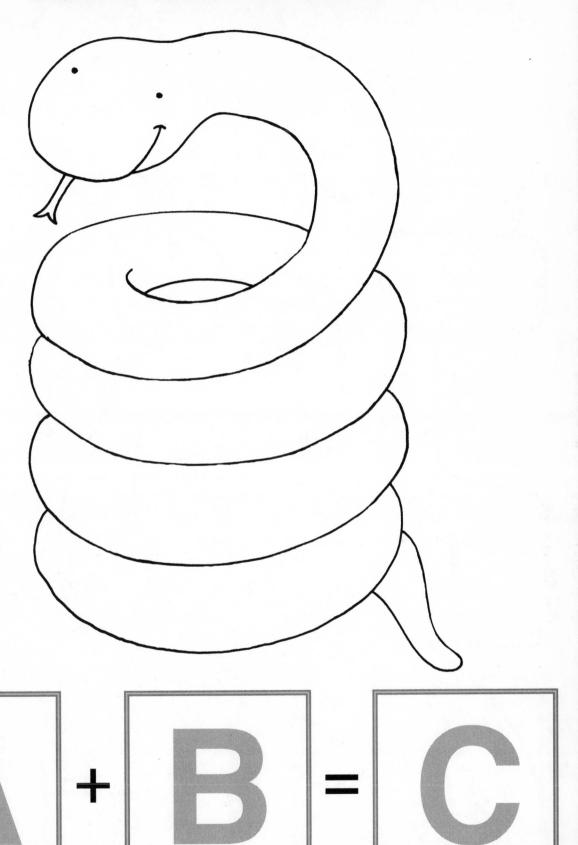

A + B = C

Animal Addition Card

A + B = C

Animal Addition Card

A + B = C

Jumpin' on Numbers

Children move Frog Cards from one Lily Pad Number Card to another to understand the concept of subtraction.

Materials

◆ Frog Cards (page 71)

◆ 2 copies of the Lily Pad Number Cards (pages 71–76)

◆ Subtraction Sheet (see "Getting Ready," right)

◆ 12- by 18-inch construction paper

* You can also use small plastic frogs instead of the Frog Cards.

Getting Ready
Sort the Lily Pad Number Cards into three groups: A (5 to 10), B (0 to 4), and C (1 to 10). Label each group. To make a Subtraction Sheet, write A–B = C on large construction paper. Make the box for each letter large enough to fit a Number Card.

Make It Simpler!
Use only Lily Pad Number Cards 3 to 5 for group A and 0 to 2 for Group B.

Challenge Them!
Have students write a subtraction problem first and show it using the Number and Frog Cards.

Jumpin' on Numbers

To Do:

1. Choose a Lily Pad Number Card from group A. Put it in box A on the Subtraction Sheet.

2. While counting, place a Frog Card on each lily pad on the Number Card.

3. Choose a Number Card from group B. Place it in box B.

4. Help the correct number of frogs "jump" from the lily pads in box A to the lily pads in box B.

5. Count how many frogs are left in box A. Place the matching Number Card in box C.

6. Do steps 1 to 5 again using different numbers.

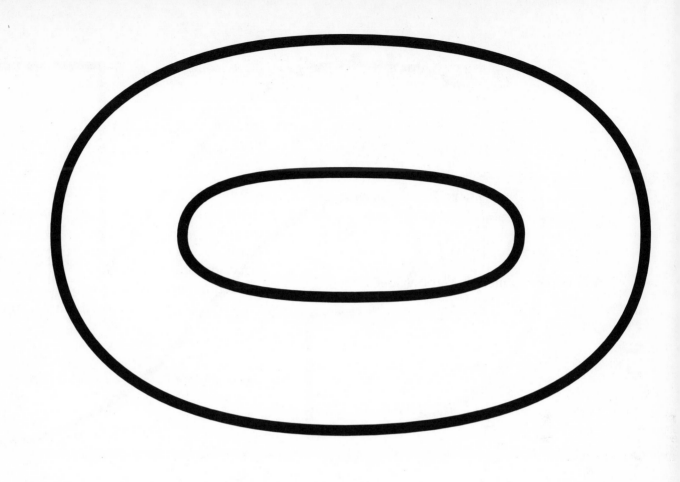

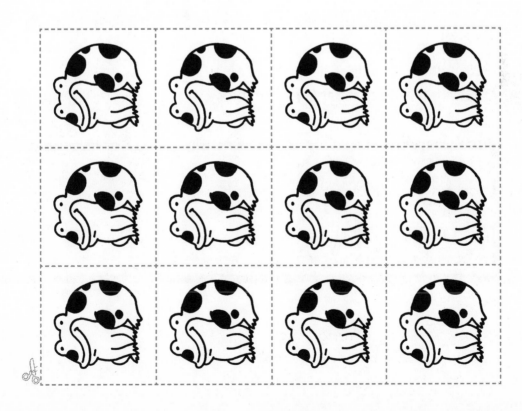

Lily Pad Number Cards

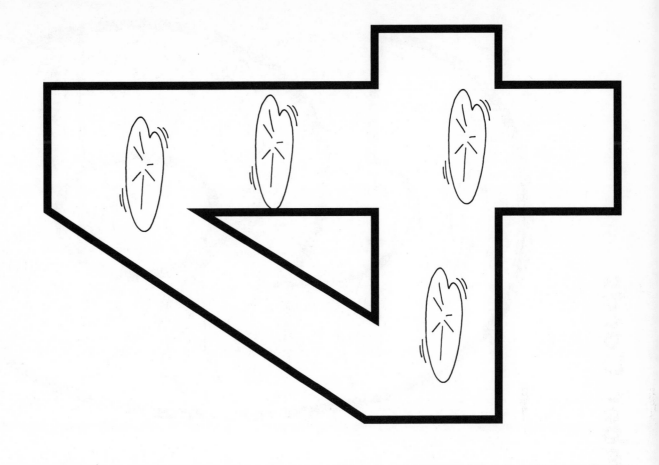

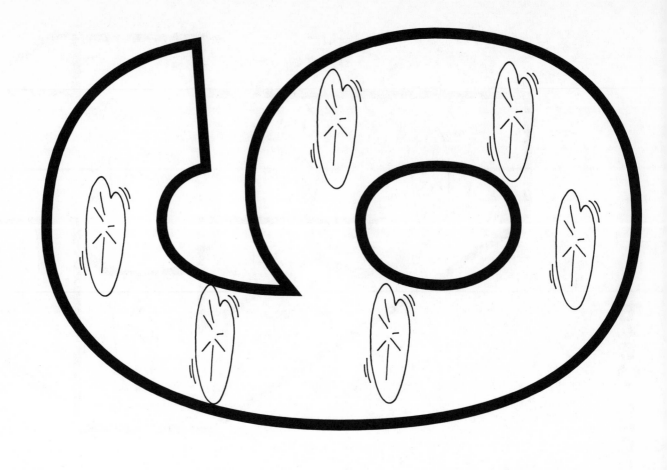

Lily Pad Number Cards

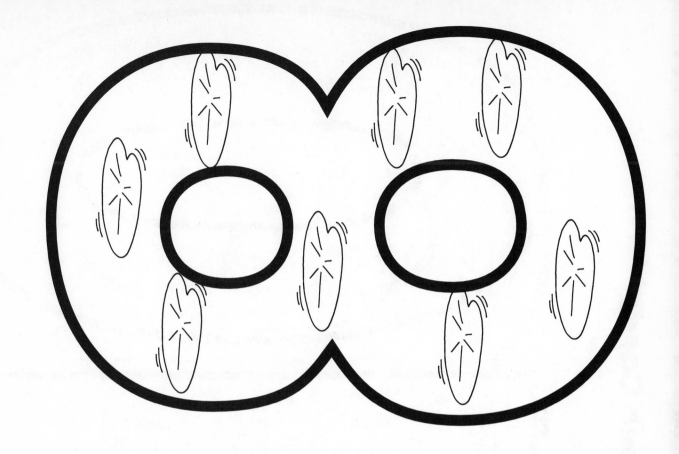

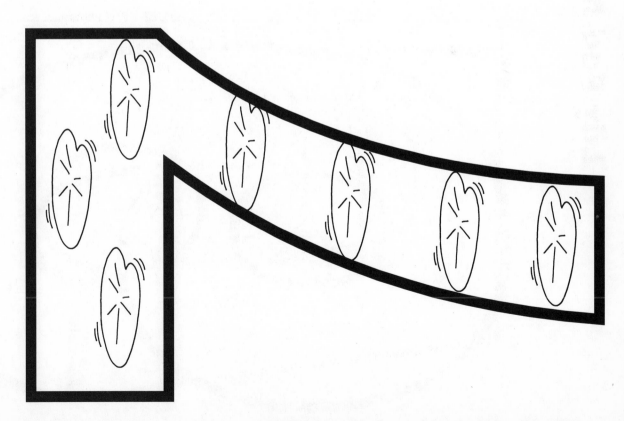

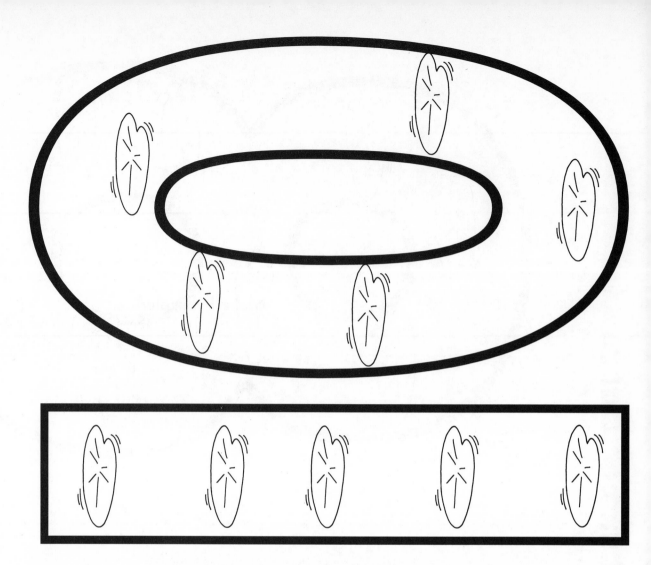

Pet Store Animals

Children pick Number Cards to see how many animals are in a pet store and how many to buy. Then, they use subtraction to find out how many animals are left in the store.

Materials

- Subtraction Mat (page 78)
- Pet Cards (pages 79–82)
- Pet Home Cards (pages 79–82)
- 2 copies of Number Cards 0 to 12 (Appendix C, pages 111–112)

Getting Ready

Sort the Number Cards into three groups: A (7 to 12), B (0 to 6), and C (0 to 12). Label each group.

Make It Simpler!

Use only the Number Cards 3 to 6 for group A, 0 to 2 for group B, and 0 to 6 for group C.

Challenge Them!

Have children write the subtraction sentence for each purchase.

Pet Store Animals

To Do:

1. Choose a pet. Place the Pet Cards and matching Pet Home Cards next to the Subtraction Mat.

2. Pick a Number Card from group A. This is the number of animals at the pet store. Put the card in box A.

3. Place that number of Pet Cards on the top part of the Pet Home Card.

4. Pick a Number Card from group B. This is the number of animals you can buy. Put the card in box B.

5. Move that number of Pet Cards from the top of the Pet Home Card to the bottom.

6. How many animals are left at the store? Place the correct Number Card in box C.

7. Do steps 1 to 6 again using another pet.

Subtraction Mat

Pet and Pet Home Cards

At the Pet Store

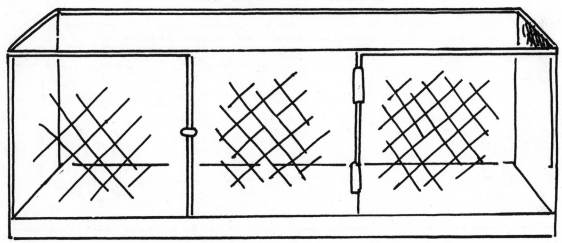

At Home

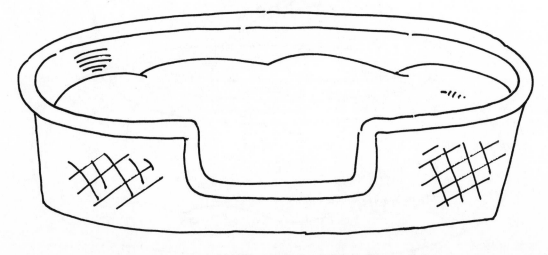

Pet and Pet Home Cards

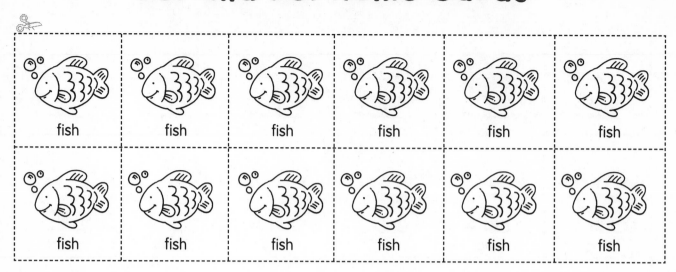

fish	fish	fish	fish	fish	fish
fish	fish	fish	fish	fish	fish

At the Pet Store

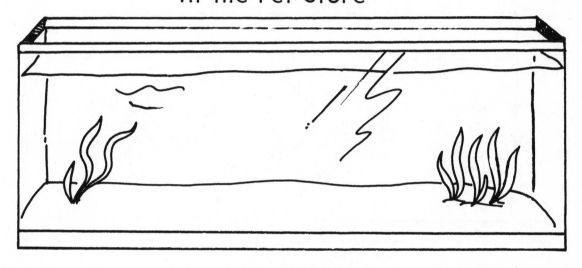

At Home

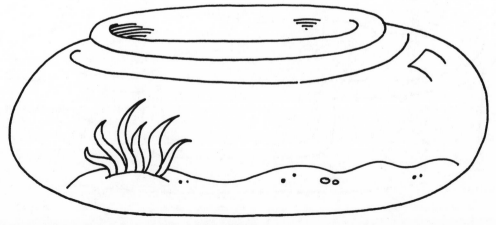

Pet and Pet Home Cards

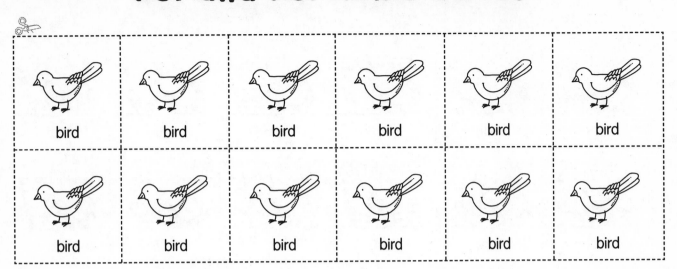

bird	bird	bird	bird	bird	bird
bird	bird	bird	bird	bird	bird

At the Pet Store

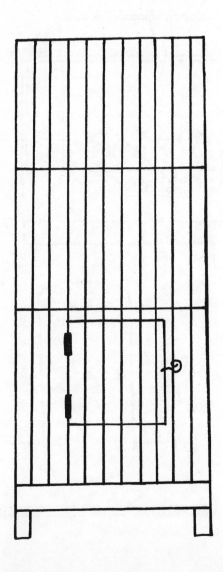

At Home

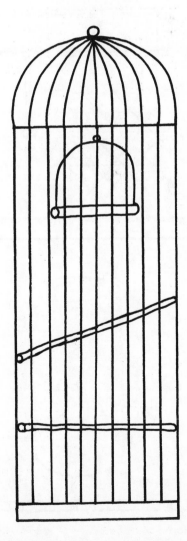

Pet and Pet Home Cards

cat   cat   cat   cat   cat   cat

cat   cat   cat   cat   cat   cat

At the Pet Store

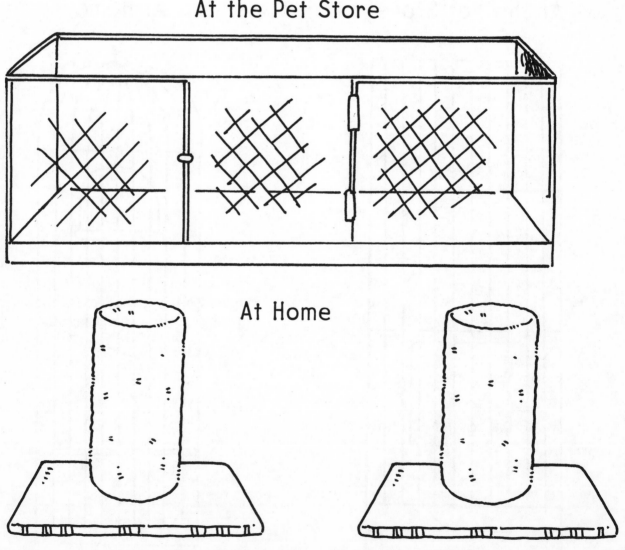

At Home

Smiles and Frowns

Children spill 10 coins on a table, then count and record how many "Smiley Faces" and "Frowny Faces" come up.

Materials

◆ 10 pennies

◆ Small cup

◆ Smiley and Frowny Faces (page 84)

◆ Face the Fractions sheet (page 85)

◆ Crayons

◆ Tape

Getting Ready
Tape the Smiley and Frowny Faces to the pennies so a face is on each side of a coin.

Make It Simpler!
Use fewer pennies to play this game. The drawing and writing of fraction steps can also be eliminated.

Challenge Them!
Play the game using more than 10 pennies. Have the children record the fraction of Smiley and Frowny faces.

Smiles and Frowns

To Do:

1. Put 10 pennies in a cup and shake it. Spill the pennies on the table.

2. Sort the pennies. Put the Smiley Faces in one group. Place the Frowny Faces in another group.

3. Count the Smiley Faces. Draw the correct number of Smiley Faces on the blank circles on the Face the Fractions sheet. Write the number on the blank space next to the smiley face at the bottom of the page.

4. Count the Frowny Faces. Draw the correct number of Frowny Faces on the sheet. Write the number on the blank space.

5. Do steps 1 to 4 again.

Smiley and Frowny Faces

Face the Fractions Sheet

How many Smiley Faces do you have?
Draw the correct number of faces below. Then write the number next to the Smiley Face. Do the same with the Frowny Faces.

$$\frac{\quad}{10}$$ =

$$\frac{\quad}{10}$$ =

$$\frac{\quad}{10}$$ =

$$\frac{\quad}{10}$$ =

$$\frac{\quad}{10}$$ =

$$\frac{\quad}{10}$$ =

$$\frac{\quad}{10}$$ =

$$\frac{\quad}{10}$$ =

Pizza Party

Children host a "pizza party" and determine how many pizza slices each guest gets.

Materials

- 10 paper plates
- Party Cards (page 87)
- Pizza Pies (pages 88–89)
- Paper clips

Getting Ready
Cut the Pizza Pies into slices. Use a paper clip to keep the slices for each Pie together.

Make It Simpler!
Use only Pizza Pies that are cut into 2, 4, and 6 pieces.

Challenge Them!
Have children draw whole Pizza Pies with toppings of their choice. When they have determined how many people are invited to the party, have them cut the pizzas into equal parts.

Pizza Party

To Do:

1. Choose a Party Card. The Party Card shows how many people are invited to the party and how many pizza slices are available.

2. Set one paper plate for each person on the table.

3. Pick the Pizza Pie with the correct number of slices.

4. Divide the Pizza Pie evenly onto each paper plate. How many slices does each person get?

5. When everyone has received food, remove the paper plates and pizza slices.

6. Do steps 1 to 5 again.

Party Cards

Pizza Pies

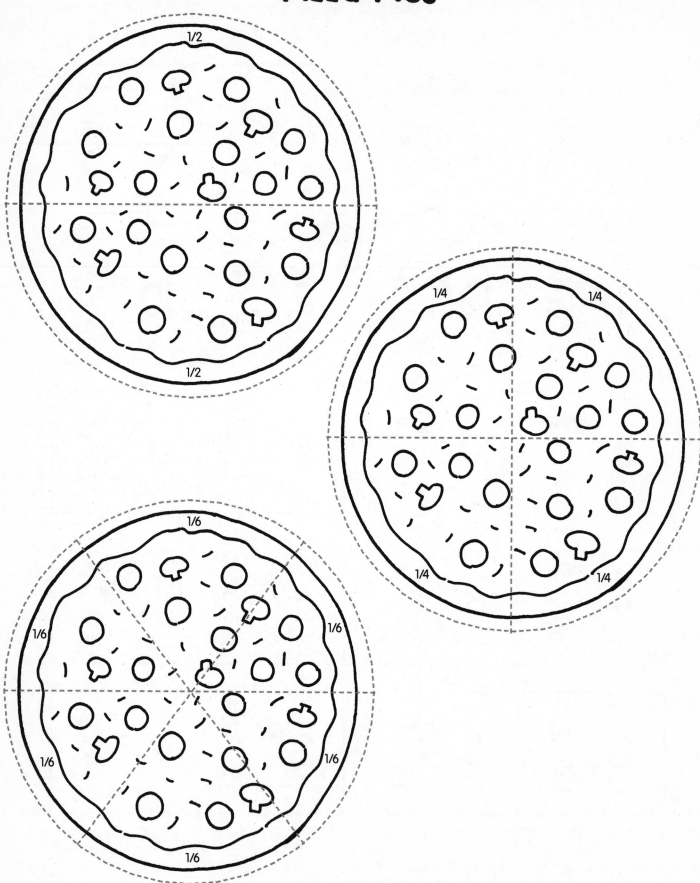

Pizza Pies

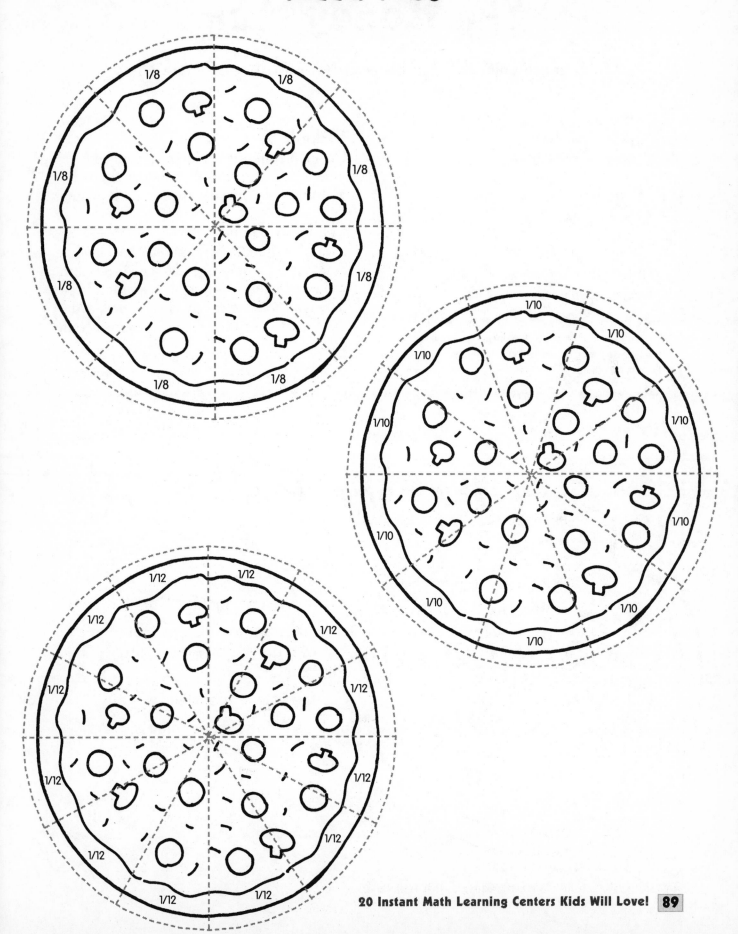

The Money Man

Children use coins to fill in blank circles on Money Picture Mats.

Materials

◆ Money Picture Mats
(pages 91–94)

◆ Quarters, dimes, nickels, and pennies*
(play money is available at most
teacher supply stores)

* To make your own play money, rub both sides of a
coin onto a sheet of paper. Cut them out and glue
the sides together. Laminate the play money to make
them more durable.

Make It Simpler!
Create pictures for children to complete
using only two coins. Provide the children
with the two coins you used in each picture.

Challenge Them!
Laminate the Money Picture Mats. Have
children use a dry-erase marker to record the
value of each coin inside its matching circle.
When all the circles have been filled, add
the total value and record it underneath the
picture.

The Money Man

To Do:

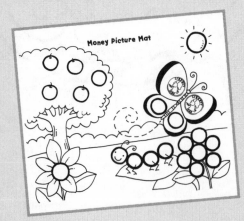

1. Choose a Money Picture Mat.

2. Find a circle on the Picture Mat.
   What coin do you think would fit
   in that circle?

3. Place the coin in the circle.

4. Do steps 2 and 3 again until all
   the circles are filled.

Money Picture Mat

cherries

pizza

lollipops

MENU

ice cream cone

cakes

Money Picture Mat

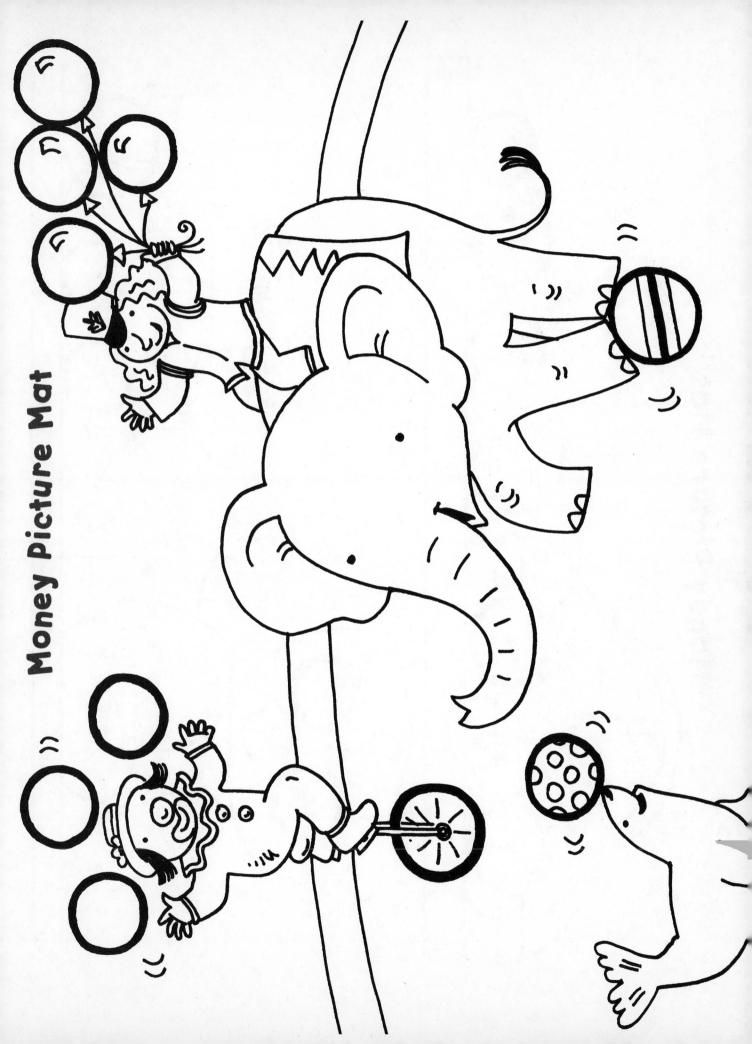

Money Picture Mat

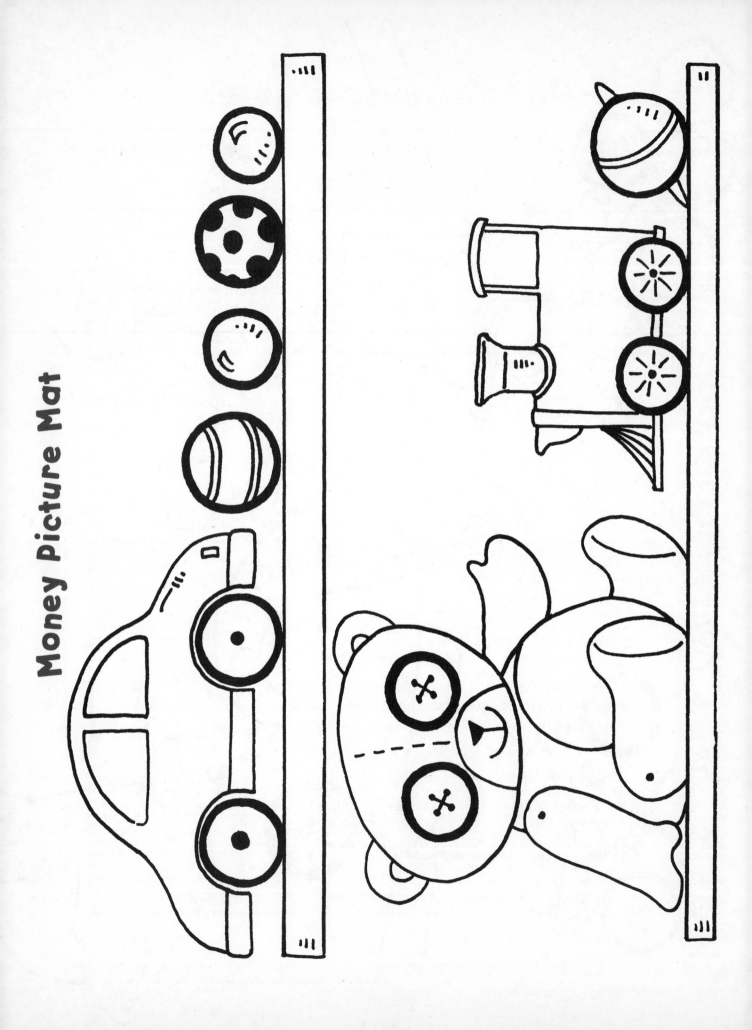

Money Picture Mat

Purchasing Power

Children figure out what coins they need to buy an item based on its Price Tag.

Materials

◆ Piggy Bank Card (page 96)

◆ Price Tags (pages 97–98)

◆ Quarters, dimes, nickels, and pennies* (play money is available at most teacher supply stores)

* To make your own play money, rub both sides of a coin onto a sheet of paper. Cut them out and glue the sides together. Laminate the play money to make them more durable.

Getting Ready
Cut apart the Price Tags.

Make It Simpler!
Tape the coins needed onto the Price Tags. The children can use this for reference.

Challenge Them!
Have children figure out other possible coin combinations to purchase the items.

Purchasing Power

To Do:

1. Put several coins on the Piggy Bank Card.

2. Pick a Price Tag. Look at the coin outlines and the price. These show what coins you need to buy the item.

3. Take the coins you need from the Piggy Bank Card. Place them on the Price Tag.

4. Do steps 2 to 3 again. If you do not have the coins to buy an item, pick another Price Tag. Keep shopping until you run out of money.

Piggy Bank Card

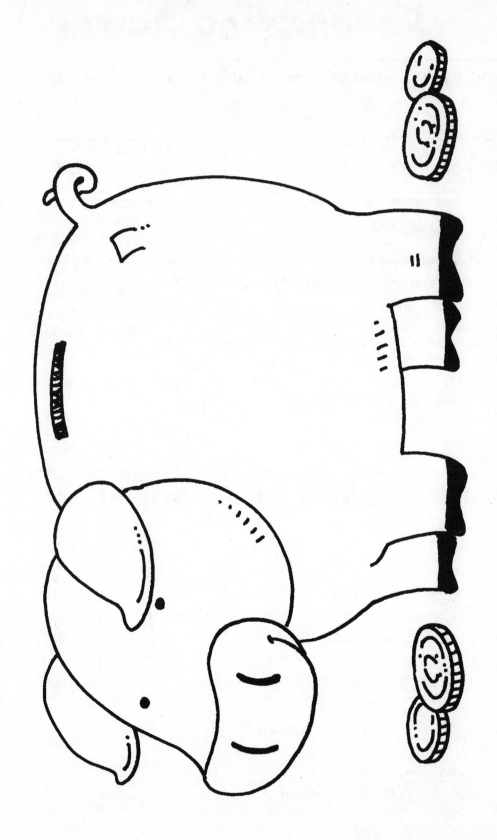

Price Tags

candy bar  25¢ 10¢ = 35¢

beach ball  25¢ 25¢ 25¢ 25¢ = $1.00

yo-yo 25¢ 25¢ 25¢ = 75¢

small bouncy ball   10¢ 10¢ 5¢ = 25¢

pencil  5¢ 1¢ 1¢ 1¢ = 8¢

car  25¢ 25¢ 1¢ 1¢ = 52¢

Price Tags

coloring boo

(25¢) (25¢) (25¢) (5¢) (1¢) (1¢) (1¢) = 83¢

candy necklace

(10¢) (10¢) (10¢) = 30¢

pack of gum

(10¢) (10¢) (1¢) (1¢) (1¢) = 23¢

sticker

(5¢) (5¢) = 10¢

ring

(5¢) (10¢) = 15¢

Watch This!

Children pick a Time Activity Card and set their clock to the time shown on the card.

Materials

- Make-a-Clock* (page 100)
- Time Activity Cards (page 101)
- Scissors
- Brads or brass paper fasteners
- Clock or watch (to serve as a model)
- Tape

* Use real watches or Judy clocks instead of paper ones.

Getting Ready
Cut apart the Time Activity Cards.

Make It Simpler!
Make the clocks beforehand.

Challenge Them!
Invite children to draw pictures of other events that happen throughout their day and set their clocks to correspond to them.

Watch This!

To Do:

1. Put together the Make-a-Clock.

2. Pick a Time Activity Card. Look at the activity and the time it happens.

3. Set your Clock so it matches the time on the card.

4. Do steps 2 and 3 again.

Make-a-Clock

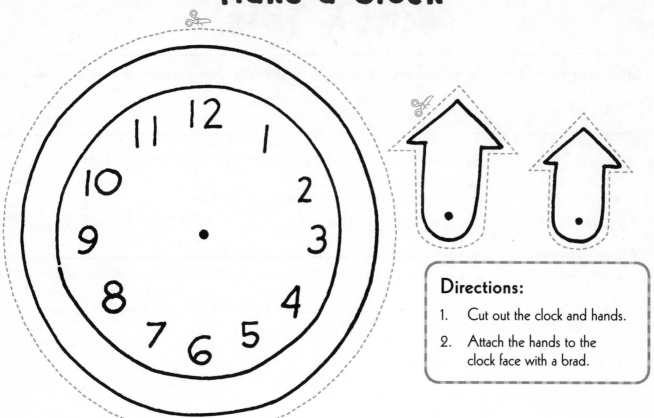

Directions:

1. Cut out the clock and hands.

2. Attach the hands to the clock face with a brad.

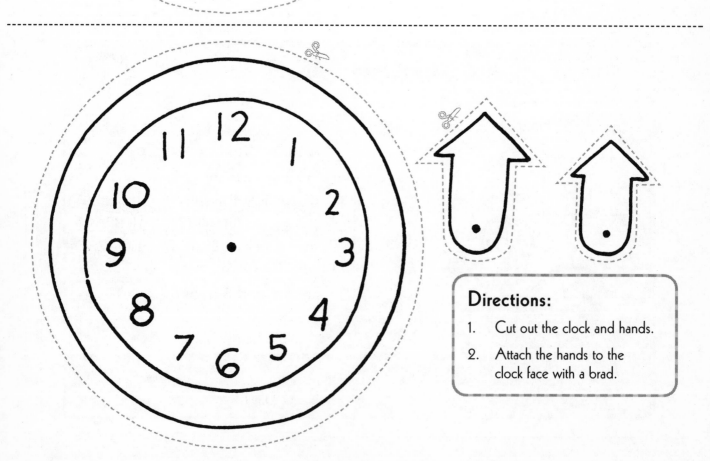

Directions:

1. Cut out the clock and hands.

2. Attach the hands to the clock face with a brad.

Time Activity Cards

Wake up

7:00 a.m.

Eat
breakfast

7:15 a.m.

Brush teeth

7:30 a.m.

School
starts

8:15 a.m.

Eat lunch

11:30 a.m.

School
gets out

2:30 p.m.

Play
outside

3:00 p.m.

Eat
dinner

5:30 p.m.

Take a bath

7:00 p.m.

Read bedtime
stories

7:30 p.m.

Brush teeth

7:45 p.m.

Go to sleep

8:00 p.m.

Time Line Settings

Children put Holiday Markers on the correct months.

Materials

◆ Calendar Pages* (pages 103–108)

◆ Holiday Markers (pages 103–108)

* You can also use an old calendar instead of the calendar templates. Take the old calendar apart.

Getting Ready
Cut apart the calendars and holiday markers.

Make It Simpler!
Present only one calendar month at a time.

Challenge Them!
Laminate the Calendar Pages and allow children to record their birthdays and other special events using dry-erase markers.

Time Line Settings

To Do:

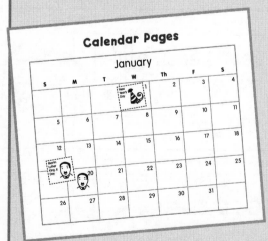

1. Put the Calendar Pages in order starting with January. Spread the pages on the table.

2. Pick a Holiday Marker. Look through the Calendar Pages. Can you find a symbol on the calendar that matches your marker?

3. Place the Marker in the correct space.

4. Do steps 2 and 3 again until all the Holiday Markers have been used.

Calendar Pages

January

S	M	T	W	Th	F	S
			1	2	3	4
5	6	7	8	9	10	11
12	13	14	15	16	17	18
19	20	21	22	23	24	25
26	27	28	29	30	31	

February

S	M	T	W	Th	F	S
						1
2	3	4	5	6	7	8
9	10	11	12	13	14	15
16	17	18	19	20	21	22
23	24	25	26	27	28	

New Year's Day

Martin Luther King Jr. Day

Chinese New Year

Lincoln's Birthday

Valentine's Day

President's Day

Washington's Birthday

Calendar Pages

March

S	M	T	W	Th	F	S
						1
2	3	4	5	6	7	8
9	10	11	12	13	14	15
16	17	18	19	20	21	22
23 / 30	24 / 31	25	26	27	28	29

April

S	M	T	W	Th	F	S
		1	2	3	4	5
6	7	8	9	10	11	12
13	14	15	16	17	18	19
20	21	22	23	24	25	26
27	28	29	30			

St. Patrick's Day

First Day of Spring

Easter

Calendar Pages

May

S	M	T	W	Th	F	S
				1	2	3
4	5	6	7	8	9	10
11	12	13	14	15	16	17
18	19	20	21	22	23	24
25	26	27	28	29	30	31

June

S	M	T	W	Th	F	S
1	2	3	4	5	6	7
8	9	10	11	12	13	14
15	16	17	18	19	20	21
22	23	24	25	26	27	28
29	30					

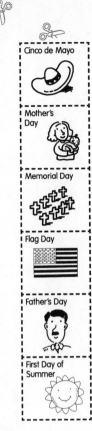

Cinco de Mayo

Mother's Day

Memorial Day

Flag Day

Father's Day

First Day of Summer

Calendar Pages

Independence Day

July

S	M	T	W	Th	F	S
		1	2	3	4	5
6	7	8	9	10	11	12
13	14	15	16	17	18	19
20	21	22	23	24	25	26
27	28	29	30	31		

August

S	M	T	W	Th	F	S
					1	2
3	4	5	6	7	8	9
10	11	12	13	14	15	16
17	18	19	20	21	22	23
24 / 31	25	26	27	28	29	30

Calendar Pages

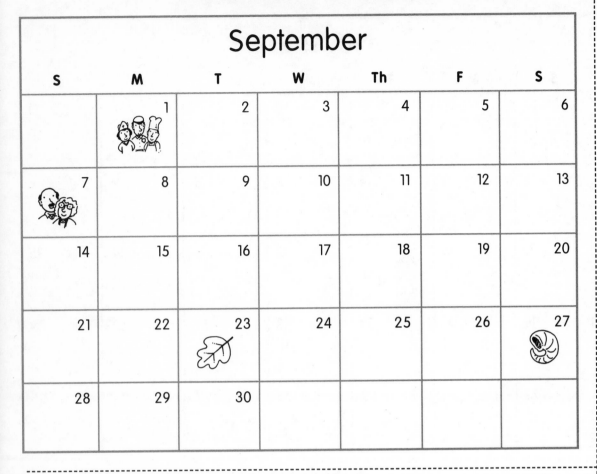

September

S	M	T	W	Th	F	S
	1	2	3	4	5	6
7	8	9	10	11	12	13
14	15	16	17	18	19	20
21	22	23	24	25	26	27
28	29	30				

October

S	M	T	W	Th	F	S
			1	2	3	4
5	6	7	8	9	10	11
12	13	14	15	16	17	18
19	20	21	22	23	24	25
26	27	28	29	30	31	

Labor Day

Grandparents Day

First Day of Fall

Rosh Hashanah

Yom Kippur

Columbus Day

Halloween

Calendar Pages

Veteran's Day

Thanksgiving Day

First Day of Hanukkah

First Day of Winter

Christmas Day

New Year's Eve

November

S	M	T	W	Th	F	S
						1
2	3	4	5	6	7	8
9	10	11	12	13	14	15
16	17	18	19	20	21	22
23 / 30	24	25	26	27	28	29

December

S	M	T	W	Th	F	S
	1	2	3	4	5	6
7	8	9	10	11	12	13
14	15	16	17	18	19	20
21	22	23	24	25	26	27
28	29	30	31			

Appendix A: Play Dough Recipe

Cooked Play Dough

You'll Need:

- 3 cups flour
- 1 1/2 cup salt
- 3 teaspoons cream of tartar
- 6 tablespoons vegetable oil
- 3 cups water
- food coloring

To Do:

1. Mix the first three ingredients in a pot.
2. Mix food coloring in the water.
3. Add the oil and colored water to the dry ingredients.
4. Put the pot on low heat and stir constantly. The dough will lump up together into one large lump.
5. Cook and stir until the dough is no longer sticky.
6. Let the dough cool completely. Keep turning it as it cools to keep it from sticking.
7. Store the cooked play dough in the refrigerator.

Uncooked Play Dough

You'll Need:

- 3 cups flour
- 1 cup salt
- 1/2 cup oil
- 1 cup water
- food coloring

To Do:

1. In a bowl, mix the first two ingredients.
2. Mix food coloring in the water.
3. Add the oil and colored water to the dry ingredients. Mix well.
4. Store the play dough in a resealable plastic bag. You don't need to refrigerate it.

Appendix B: Shape Cards

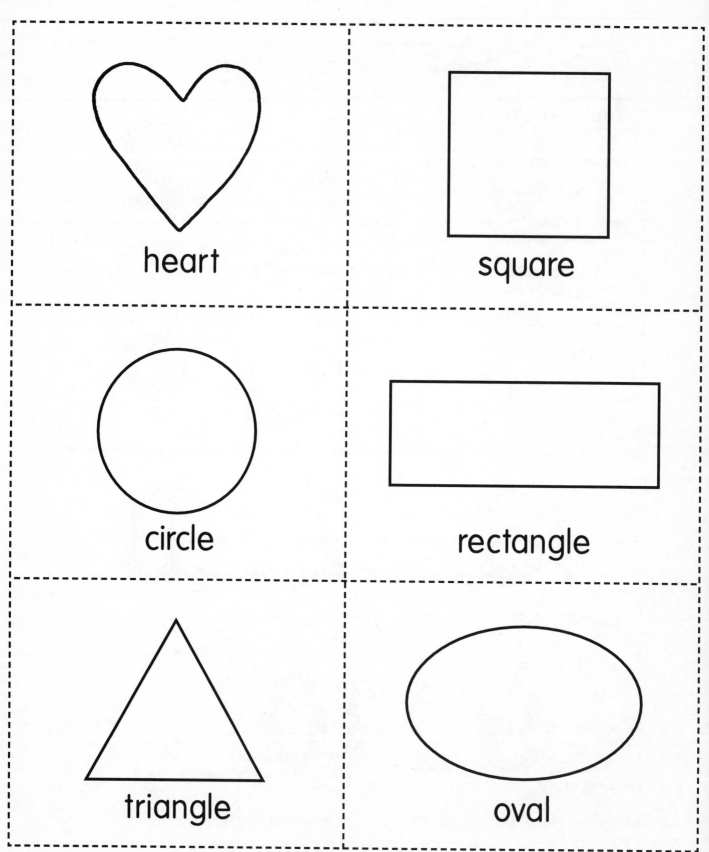

heart

square

circle

rectangle

triangle

oval

Appendix C: Number Cards

0 1 2

3 4 5

6 7 8

9 10

11	**12**	**13**
14	**15**	**16**
17	**18**	**19**
	20	